The One Minute Manager

Also available

Putting the One Minute Manager to Work
Kenneth Blanchard, Ph.D. and Robert Lorber, Ph.D. (1984)
The One Minute Sales Person
Spencer Johnson, M.D. and Larry Wilson (1985)
Leadership and the One Minute Manager
Kenneth Blanchard, Ph.D., Patricia Zigarmi, Ed.D.
and Drea Zigarmi, Ed.D.

The One Minute Manager

Kenneth Blanchard, Ph.D.
Spencer Johnson, M.D.

HarperCollins *Publishers* India
a joint venture with

New Delhi

HarperCollins *Publishers* India
a joint venture with
The India Today Group
1A Hamilton House, Connaught Place, New Delhi 110 001, India

First published in 1992 by
HarperCollins *Publishers* India
Twentieth impression 2003

HarperCollins *Publishers*
1A Hamilton House, Connaught Place, New Delhi 110 001, India
77-85 Fulham Palace Road, London W6 8JB, United Kingdom
Hazelton Lanes, 55 Avenue Road, Suite 2900, Toronto, Ontario M5R 3L2
and 1995 Markham Road, Scarborough, Ontario M1B 5M8, Canada
25 Ryde Road, Pymble, Sydney, NSW 2073, Australia
31 View Road, Glenfield, Auckland 10, New Zealand
10 East 53rd Street, New York NY 10022, USA

Printed and bound at
Thomson Press (India) Ltd.

:01 *The Symbol*

The One Minute Manager's symbol - a one minute readout from the face of a modern digital watch - is intended to remind each of us to take a minute out of our day to look into the faces of the people we manage. And to realize that *they* are our most important resources.

Contents

:01

Introduction

In this brief story, we present you with a great deal of what we have learned from our studies in medicine and in the behavioural sciences about how people work best with other people.

By 'best', we mean how people produce valuable results, and feel good about themselves, the organization and the other people with whom they work.

This allegory, *The One Minute Manager*, is a simple compilation of what many wise people have taught us and what we have learned ourselves. We recognize the importance of these sources of wisdom. We also realize that the people who work with you as their manager will look to you as one of *their* sources of wisdom.

We trust, therefore, that you will take the practical knowledge you gain from this book and use it in your daily management. For as the ancient sage, Confucius, advises each of us: 'The essence of knowledge is, having it, to use it'.

We hope you enjoy *using* what you learn from *The One Minute Manager* and that, as a result, you and the people you work with will enjoy healthier, happier and more productive lives.

Kenneth Blanchard, Ph.D.
Spencer Johnson, M.D.

:01 *The One Minute Manager*

ONCE there was a bright young man who was looking for an effective manager.

He wanted to work for one. He wanted to become one.

His search had taken him over many years to the far corners of the world.

He had been in small towns and in the capitals of powerful nations.

He had spoken with many managers: with government administrators and military officers, construction superintendents and corporate executives, university professors and shop stewards, with the managers of shops and stores, of restaurants, banks and hotels, with men and women - young and old.

He had gone into every kind of office, large and small, luxurious and sparse, with windows and without.

He was beginning to see the full spectrum of how people manage people.

But he wasn't always pleased with what he saw.

He had seen many 'tough' managers whose organizations seemed to win while their people lost.

Some of their superiors thought they were good managers.

Many of their subordinates thought otherwise.

As the man sat in each of these 'tough people's' offices, he asked, 'What kind of a manager would you say you are?'

Their answers varied only slightly.

'I'm an autocratic manager – I keep on top of the situation', he was told. 'A bottom-line manager.' 'Hard-nosed.' 'Realistic.' 'Profit-minded.'

He heard the pride in their voices and their interest in results.

The man also met many 'nice' managers whose people seemed to win while their organizations lost.

Some of the people who reported to them thought they were good managers.

Those to whom they reported had their doubts.

As the man sat and listened to these 'nice' people answer the same question, he heard:

'I'm a democratic manager'. 'Participative.' 'Supportive.' 'Considerate.' 'Humanistic.'

He heard the pride in their voices and their interest in people.

But he was disturbed.

It was as though most managers in the world were primarily interested either in results or in people.

The managers who were interested in results often seemed to be labelled 'autocratic', while the managers interested in people were often labelled 'democratic'.

The young man thought each of these managers – the 'tough' autocrat and the 'nice' democrat – were only partially effective. 'It's like being half a manager', he thought.

He returned home tired and discouraged.

He might have given up his search long ago, but he had one great advantage. He knew exactly what he was looking for.

'Effective managers', he thought, 'manage themselves and the people they work with so that both the organization and the people profit from their presence'.

The young man had looked everywhere for an effective manager but had found only a few. The few he did find would not share their secrets with him. He began to think maybe he would never find out what really made an effective manager tick.

Then he began hearing marvellous stories about a special manager who lived, ironically, in a nearby town. He heard that people liked to work for this man and that they produced great results together. The young man wondered if the stories were really true and, if so, whether this manager would be willing to share his secrets with him.

Curious, he telephoned the special manager's secretary for an appointment. The secretary put him through immediately.

The young man asked this special manager when he could see him. He heard, 'Any time this week is fine, except Wednesday morning. You pick the time.'

The young man quietly chuckled because this supposedly marvellous manager sounded very strange to him. What kind of manager had that kind of time available? But the young man was fascinated. He went to see him.

WHEN the young man arrived at the manager's office, he found him standing and looking out of the window. When the young man coughed, the manager turned and smiled. He invited the young man to sit down and asked, 'What can I do for you?'

The young man said, 'I'd like to ask you some questions about how you manage people'.

The manager willingly said, 'Fire away'.

'Well, to begin with, do you hold regularly scheduled meetings with your subordinates?'

'Yes, I do - once a week on Wednesdays from 9:00 until 11:00. That's why I couldn't see you then', responded the manager.

'What do you do at those meetings?' probed the young man.

'I listen while my people review and analyse what they accomplished last week, the problems they had, and what still needs to be accomplished. Then we develop plans and strategies for the next week.'

'Are the decisions made at those meetings binding on both you and your staff?' questioned the young man.

'Of course they are', insisted the manager. 'What would be the point of having the meeting if they weren't?'

'Then you are a participative manager, aren't you?' asked the young man.

'On the contrary', insisted the manager, 'I don't believe in participating in any of my staff's decision-making'.

'Then what is the purpose of your meetings?'

'I already told you that', he said. 'Please, young man, do not ask me to repeat myself. It is a waste of my time and yours.

'We're here to get results', the manager continued. 'The purpose of this organization is efficiency. By being organized we are a great deal more productive.'

'Oh, so you're aware of the need for productivity. Then you're more results-oriented than people-oriented', the young man suggested.

'No!' the manager retorted, startling his visitor. 'I hear that all too often.' He got to his feet and began to walk about. 'How on earth can I get results if it's not through people? I care about people *and* results. They go hand in hand.

'Here, young man, look at this.' The manager handed his visitor a plaque. 'I keep it on my desk to remind me of a practical truth.'

*

People Who Feel Good About Themselves

Produce Good Results

*

As the young man looked at the plaque, the manager said, 'Think about yourself. When do you work best? Is it when you feel good about yourself? Or when you don't?'

The young man nodded as he began to see the obvious. 'I get more done when I'm feeling good about myself', he responded.

'Of course you do', the manager agreed. 'And so does everyone else.'

The young man raised his index finger with new-found insight. 'So', he said, 'helping people to feel good about themselves is a key to getting more done'.

'Yes', the manager agreed. 'However, remember productivity is more than just the *quantity* of work done. It is also the *quality*.' He walked over to the window and said, 'Come over here, young man'.

He pointed to the traffic below and asked, 'Do you see how many foreign cars there are on the road?'

The young man looked out of the window and said, 'I see more of them every day. And I suppose that's because they're more economical and they last longer.'

The manager nodded reluctantly and said 'Exactly. So why do you think people are buying foreign cars? Because our manufacturers did not make *enough* cars? Or', the manager said without interrupting, 'because they did not make the *quality* car the public really wanted?'

'Now that I think of it', the young man answered, 'it's a question of *quality* and *quantity*'.

'Of course', the manager added. 'Quality is simply giving people the product or service they really want and need.'

The older man stood at the window lost in his thoughts. He could remember, not so long ago, when Britain and America provided the technology that helped to rebuild Europe and Asia. It still amazed him that they had fallen so far behind in productivity.

The young man broke the manager's concentration. 'I'm reminded of an ad I saw on television', the visitor volunteered. 'It showed the name of the foreign car, and over it came the words *If you're going to take out a long-term car loan, don't buy a short-term car.*'

The manager turned and said quietly, 'I'm afraid that's a rather good summary. And that's the whole point. Productivity is both quantity and quality.'

The manager and his visitor began to walk back towards their chairs. 'And frankly, the best way to achieve both of these results is through people.'

The young man's interest increased. As he sat down, he asked, 'Well, you've already said that you're not a participative manager. Just how would you describe *yourself*?'

'That's easy', he responded without hesitation. 'I'm a One Minute Manager.'

The young man's face showed surprise. He'd never heard of a One Minute Manager. 'You're a what?'

The manager laughed and said, 'I'm a One Minute Manager. I call myself that because it takes very little time for me to get very big results from people.'

Although the young man had spoken with many managers, he had never heard one talk like this. It was hard to believe. A One Minute Manager – someone who gets good results without taking much time.

Seeing the doubt on his face the manager said, 'You don't believe me, do you? You don't believe that I'm a One Minute Manager.'

'I must admit it's hard for me even to imagine', the young man responded.

The manager laughed and said, 'Listen, you'd better talk to my staff if you really want to know what kind of manager I am'.

The manager leaned over and spoke into the office intercom. His secretary, Ms. Metcalfe, came in moments later and handed the young man a sheet of paper.

'Those are the names, positions and phone numbers of the six people who report to me', the One Minute Manager explained.

'Which ones should I talk to?' the young man asked.

'That's your decision', the manager replied. 'Pick any name. Talk to any one of them or all of them.'

'Well, I mean who should I start with?'

'I already told you, I don't make decisions for other people', the manager said firmly. 'Make that decision yourself.' He stood up and walked his visitor towards the door.

'You have asked me, not once, but twice, to make a simple decision for you. Frankly, young man, I find that annoying. Do not ask me to repeat myself. Either pick a name and get started, or take your search for effective management elsewhere.'

The visitor was stunned. He felt uncomfortable, very uncomfortable. A moment of embarrassed silence seemed like an eternity.

Then the One Minute Manager looked the young man in the eye and said, 'You want to know about managing people, and I admire that'. He shook his visitor's hand.

'If you have any questions after talking to some of my people', he said warmly, 'come back and see me. I appreciate your interest and desire to learn how to manage. I would, in fact, like to give you the concept of the One Minute Manager as a gift. Someone gave it to me once and it's made all the difference to me. I want you to understand it fully. If you like it, you may want to become a One Minute Manager yourself someday.'

'Thank you', the young man managed.

He left the manager's office somewhat dumbfounded. As he passed the secretary she said understandingly, 'I can see from your dazed look that you've already experienced our One Minute Manager'.

The young man said very slowly, still trying to work things out, 'I rather think I have'.

'Maybe I can help you', Ms. Metcalfe said. 'I've phoned the six people who report to him. Five of them are here and they have each agreed to see you. You may be better able to understand our One Minute Manager after you've spoken with them.'

The young man thanked her, looked over the list and decided to talk to three of them: Mr. Trenell, Mr. Levy and Ms. Brown.

WHEN the young man arrived at Trenell's office, he found a middle-aged man smiling at him. 'Well, you've been to see the "old man". He's quite a character, isn't he?'

'He seems that way', the young man responded.

'Did he tell you about being a One Minute Manager?'

'He certainly did. It's not true, is it?' asked the young man.

'You'd better believe it is. I hardly ever see him.'

'You mean you never get any help from him?' asked the puzzled young man.

'Essentially very little, although he does spend some time with me at the beginning of a new task or responsibility. That's when he does One Minute Goal Setting.'

'One Minute Goal Setting. What's that?' said the young man. 'He told me he was a One Minute Manager, but he didn't say anything about One Minute Goal Setting.'

'That's the first of the three secrets to One Minute Management', Trenell answered.

'Three secrets?' the young man asked, wanting to know more.

'Yes', said Trenell. 'One Minute Goal Setting is the first one and the foundation for One Minute Management. You see, in most organizations when you ask people what they do and then ask their boss, all too often you get two different lists. In fact, in some organizations I've worked in, any relationship between what I thought my job responsibilities were and what my boss thought they were was purely coincidental. And then I would get in trouble for not doing something I didn't even think was my job.'

'Does that ever happen here?' asked the young man.

'No!' Trenell said. 'It never happens here. The One Minute Manager always makes it clear what our responsibilities are and what we are being held accountable for.'

'Just how does he do that?' the young man wanted to know.

'Efficiently', Trenell said with a smile.

Trenell began to explain. 'Once he has told me what needs to be done or we have agreed on what needs to be done, then each goal is recorded on no more than a single page. The One Minute Manager feels that a goal, and its performance standard, should take no more than 250 words to express. He insists that anyone be able to read it within a minute. He keeps a copy and I keep a copy so everything is clear and so we can both periodically check the progress.'

'Do you have these one-page statements for every goal?'

'Yes', answered Trenell.

'Well, wouldn't there be a lot of these one-page statements for each person?'

'No, there really aren't', Trenell insisted. 'The old man believes in the 80–20 goal-setting rule. That is, 80 per cent of your really important results will come from 20 per cent of your goals. So we only do One Minute Goal Setting on that 20 per cent; that is, our key areas of responsibility – maybe three to six goals in all. Of course, in the event a special project comes up, we set special One Minute Goals.'

'Interesting', the young man commented. 'I think I understand the importance of One Minute Goal Setting. It sounds like a philosophy of "no surprises" - everyone knows what is expected from the beginning.'

'Exactly', Trenell agreed.

'So is One Minute Goal Setting just understanding what your responsibilities are?' the young man asked.

'No. Once we know what our job is, the manager always makes sure we know what good performance is. In other words, performance standards are clear. He shows us what he expects.'

'How does he show you what he expects?' asked the young man.

'Let me give you an example', Trenell suggested.

'One of my One Minute Goals was this: identify performance problems and come up with solutions which, when implemented, will turn the situation around.

'When I first came to work here I spotted a problem that needed to be solved, but I didn't know what to do. So I called the One Minute Manager. When he answered the phone, I said, *I find I have a problem.* Before I could get another word out, he said, *Good! That's what you've been hired to solve.* Then there was a dead silence on the other end of the phone.

'I didn't know what to do. The silence was deafening. I eventually stuttered out, *But I don't know how to solve this problem.*

'*Trenell,* he said, *one of your goals for the future is for you to identify and solve your own problems. But since you are new, come up here and we'll talk.*

'When I got up there, he said, *Tell me, Trenell, what your problem is – but put it in behavioural terms.*

'*Behavioural terms?* I echoed. *What do you mean by behavioural terms?*

'*I mean,* the manager explained to me, *that I do not want to hear about only attitudes or feelings. Tell me what is happening in observable, measurable terms.*

'I described the problem as best I could.

'He said, *That's good, Trenell! Now tell me what you would like to be happening in behavioural terms.*

'*I don't know*, I said.

'*Then don't waste my time,* he snapped.

'I just froze in amazement for a few seconds. I didn't know what to do. He mercifully broke the dead silence.

'*If you can't tell me what you'd like to be happening,* he said, *you don't have a problem yet. You're just complaining. A problem exists only if there is a difference between what is* actually *happening and what you* desire *to be happening.*

'Being a quick learner, I suddenly realized I knew what I wanted to be happening. After I told him, he asked me to talk about what may have caused the discrepancy between the actual and the desired.

'After that the One Minute Manager said, *Well, what are you going to do about it?*'

'*Well, I could do A,* I said.

'*If you did A, would what you want to happen actually happen?* he asked.

'*No,* I said.

'*Then you have a very bad solution. What else could you do?* he asked.

'*I could do B,* I said.

'*But if you do B, will what you want to happen really happen?* he countered again.

'*No,* I realized.

'*Then, that's also a bad solution,* he said. *What elsc can you do?*

'I thought about it for a couple of minutes and said, *I could do C. But if I do C, what I want to happen won't happen, so that is a bad solution, isn't it?*

'*Right. You're starting to come around,* the manager then said, with a smile on his face. *Is there anything else you could do?* he asked.

'*Maybe I could combine some of these solutions,* I said.

'*That sounds worth trying,* he said.

'*In fact, if I do A this week, B next week and C in two weeks, I'll have it solved. That's fantastic. Thanks so much. You solved my problem for me.*

'He got very annoyed. *I did not,* he interrupted, *you solved it yourself. I just asked you questions – questions you are able to ask yourself. Now get out of here and start solving your own problems on your time, not mine.*

'I knew what he had done, of course. He'd shown me how to solve problems so that I could do it on my own in the future.

'Then he stood, looked me straight in the eye and said, *You're good, Trenell. Remember that the next time you have a problem.*

'I remember smiling as I left his office.'

Trenell leaned back in his chair and looked as if he were reliving his first encounter with the One Minute Manager.

'So', the young man began, reflecting on what he had just heard . . .

One Minute Goal Setting is simply:

1. Agree on your goals.
2. See what good behaviour looks like.
3. Write out each of your goals on a single sheet of paper using less than 250 words.
4. Read and re-read each goal, which requires only a minute or so each time you do it.
5. Take a minute every once in a while out of your day to look at your performance, and
6. See whether or not your behaviour matches your goal.

'That's it', Trenell exclaimed, 'you're a fast learner'.

'Thank you', the young man said, feeling good about himself. 'But let me just jot that down', he said, 'I want to remember that'.

After the young man wrote briefly in the small blue notebook he carried with him, he leaned forward and asked, 'If One Minute Goal Setting is the first secret to becoming a One Minute Manager, what are the other two?'

Trenell smiled, looked at his watch and said, 'Why don't you ask Levy that? You're scheduled to see him this morning too, aren't you?'

The young man was amazed. How did Trenell know that? 'Yes', the young man said as he rose to shake Trenell's hand. 'Thanks so much for your time.'

'You're welcome'. Trenell replied. 'Time is one thing I have a lot more of now. As you can probably tell, I'm becoming a One Minute Manager myself.'

AS the young man left Trenell's office, he was struck by the simplicity of what he had heard. He thought, 'It certainly makes sense. After all, how can you be an effective manager unless you and your people are sure of what they are being asked to do? And what an efficient way to do it.'

The young man walked the length of the building and took the lift to the second floor. When he got to Mr. Levy's office, he was surprised to meet so young a man. Levy was probably in his late 20s or early 30s. 'Well, you've been to see the "old man". He's quite a character, isn't he?'

He was already getting used to the One Minute Manager being called 'quite a character'.

'I reckon he is', responded the young man.

'Did he tell you about being a One Minute Manager?' asked Levy.

'He certainly did. It's not true, is it?' asked the young man, wondering if he'd get a different answer from Trenell's.

'You'd better believe it's true. I hardly ever see him.'

'You mean you never get any help from him?' asked the young man.

'Essentially very little, although he does spend a fair amount of time with me at the beginning of a new task or responsibility.'

'Yes, I know about One Minute Goal Setting', interrupted the young man.

'Actually I wasn't thinking so much about One Minute Goal Setting. I was referring to One Minute Praisings.'

'One Minute Praisings?' echoed the young man. 'Are they the second secret to becoming a One Minute Manager?'

'Yes, they are', Levy revealed. 'In fact, when I first started to work here, the One Minute Manager made it very clear to me what he was going to do.'

'What was that?' the visitor asked.

'He said that he knew that it would be a lot easier for me to do well, if I got crystal-clear feedback from him on how I was doing.

'He said he wanted me to succeed. He wanted me to be a big help to the organization, and to enjoy my work.

'He told me that he would try, therefore, to let me know *in no uncertain terms* when I was doing well, and when I was doing poorly.

'And then he cautioned me that it might not be very comfortable at first for either of us.'

'Why?' the visitor asked.

'Because, as he pointed out to me then, most managers don't manage that way and people aren't used to it. Then he assured me that such feedback would be a big help to me.

'Can you give me an example of what you are talking about?' the young man requested.

'Of course', Levy said. 'Shortly after I started to work, I noticed that, after my manager had done One Minute Goal Setting with me, he would stay in close contact.'

'What do you mean by "close contact"?' asked the young man.

'There were two ways that he did it', explained Levy. 'First of all, he observed my activities very closely. He never seemed to be very far away. Secondly, he made me keep detailed records of my progress which he insisted I send to him.'

'That's interesting', said the young man. 'Why does he do that?'

'At first I thought he was spying and didn't trust me. That is, until I found out from some of the other people who report to him what he was really doing.'

'What was that?' the young man wanted to know.

'He was trying to catch me doing something right', Levy said.

'Catch you doing something right?' echoed the young man.

'Yes', replied Levy. 'We have a motto around here that says:

*

Help People
Reach Their
Full Potential

Catch Them
Doing Something
Right

*

Levy continued, 'In most organizations the managers spend most of their time catching people doing – what?' he asked the young man.

The young man smiled and said knowingly, 'Doing something wrong'.

'Right!' said Levy. 'Here we put the accent on the positive. We catch people doing something *right*.'

The young man made a few notes in his notebook and then asked, 'What happens, Mr. Levy, when the One Minute Manager catches you doing something right?'

'That's when he gives you a One Minute Praising', Levy said with a smile.

'What does that mean?' the young man wanted to know.

'Well, when he has seen that you have done something right, he comes over and makes contact with you. That often includes putting his hand on your shoulder or briefly touching you in a friendly way.'

'Doesn't it bother you when he touches you?' the young man wondered.

'No!' Levy insisted. 'On the contrary, it helps. I know he really cares about me and he wants me to prosper. As he says, "The more consistently successful your people are, the higher you rise in the organization".

'When he makes contact, it's brief, but it lets me know once again that we're really on the same side.

'Anyway, after that', Levy continued, 'he looks you straight in the eye and tells you precisely what you did right. Then he shares with you how good he feels about what you did.'

'I don't think I've ever heard of a manager doing that', the young man broke in. 'That must make you feel pretty good.'

'It certainly does', Levy confirmed, 'for several reasons. First of all, I get a praising as soon as I've done something right.' He smiled and leaned towards his visitor. Then he laughed and said, 'I don't have to wait for an annual performance review, if you know what I mean'. Both men smiled.

'Second, since he specifies exactly what I did right, I know he's sincere and familiar with what I am doing. Third, he is consistent.'

'Consistent?' echoed the young man, wanting to know more.

'Yes', insisted Levy. 'He will praise me if I am performing well and deserve it even if things are not going well for him elsewhere. I know he may be annoyed about other things. But he responds to my situation, not according to what's going on elsewhere for him at the time. And I really appreciate that.'

'Doesn't all this praising have to take up a lot of the manager's time?' the young man asked.

'Not really', said Levy. 'Remember you don't have to praise someone for very long for them to know you noticed and you care. It usually takes less than a minute.'

'And that's why it's called a One Minute Praising', the visitor said, as he wrote down what he was learning.

'Right', Levy said.

'Is he always trying to catch you doing something right?' the young man asked.

'No, of course not', Levy answered. 'Just when you first start work here or when you begin a new project or responsibility, then he does. After you get to know the ropes, he doesn't seem to be around much.'

'Why?' the young man wondered.

'Because you and he have other ways of knowing when your job performance is "praiseworthy". You both can review the data in the information system – the sales figures, expenditures, production schedules, and so on. And then', Levy added, 'after a while you begin to catch yourself doing things right and you start praising yourself. Also, you're always wondering when he might praise you again and that seems to keep you going even when he's not around. It's uncanny. I've never worked so hard at a job in my life.'

'That's really interesting', commented the young man. 'So One Minute Praising is a secret to becoming a One Minute Manager.'

'It is, indeed', Levy said with a gleam in his eye. He enjoyed watching someone learn the secrets of One Minute Management.

As the visitor looked at his notes, he quickly reviewed what he had learned about the One Minute Praising.

The One Minute Praising works well when you:

1. Tell people *right from the start* that you are going to let them know how they are doing.
2. Praise people immediately.
3. Tell people what they did right – be specific.
4. Tell people how good you feel about what they did right, and how it helps the organization and the other people who work there.
5. Stop for a moment of silence to let them *'feel'* how good you feel.
6. Encourage them to do more of the same.
7. Shake hands or touch people in a way that makes it clear that you support their success in the organization.

'What's the third secret?' the young man asked anxiously.

Levy laughed at the visitor's enthusiasm, rose from his chair and said, 'Why don't you ask Ms. Brown? I understand you're planning to talk to her, too.'

'Yes, I am', admitted the young man. 'Well, thanks so much for your time.'

'That's OK', insisted Levy. 'Time is one thing I have plenty of – you see, I'm a One Minute Manager myself now.'

The visitor smiled. He'd heard that somewhere before.

He wanted to reflect on what he was learning. He left the building and took a walk in a nearby park. He was struck again by the simplicity and common sense of what he had heard. 'You can't argue with the effectiveness of catching people doing something right', the young man thought, 'especially after they *know* what they are to do and what good performance looks like.

'But do One Minute Praisings really work?' he wondered. 'Does all this One Minute Management stuff really get results – bottom-line results?'

As he walked along his curiosity about results increased. So he returned to the One Minute Manager's secretary and asked Ms. Metcalfe to reschedule his appointment with Ms. Brown for some time the next morning.

'Tomorrow morning is fine', the secretary said as she put down the phone. 'Ms. Brown said to tell you to come any time except Wednesday morning.'

Then she rang another extension to make the new appointment he requested. He was to see Ms. Jones, an official at head office. 'They have information there about all the different plants and locations in the whole company', Ms. Metcalfe said in a very knowing way. 'I'm sure you'll find whatever you're looking for.' He thanked her and left.

AFTER lunch the young man went to his appointment at head office. There he met Ms. Jones, a competent looking woman in her early 40s. Getting down to business, the young man asked, 'Could you please tell me which of all your operations in the country is the most efficient and effective? I want to compare it with the so-called One Minute Manager's.'

A moment later, he laughed, as he heard Ms. Jones say, 'Well, you won't have to look very far, because it *is* the One Minute Manager's. He's quite a character, isn't he? His operation is the most efficient and effective of all of our plants.'

'That's unbelievable', said the young man. 'Does he have the best equipment?'

'No', said Ms. Jones. 'In fact, he's got some of the oldest.'

'Well, there's got to be something wrong there', said the young man, still puzzled by the old man's management style. 'Tell me, does he lose a lot of his people? Does he have a lot of turnover?'

'Come to think of it', Ms. Jones said, 'he does have a lot of turnover'.

'Aha', the young man said, thinking he was on to something.

'What happens to those people when they leave the One Minute Manager?' the young man wanted to know.

'We give them their own operation', Ms. Jones quickly responded. 'After two years with him, they say, "Who needs a manager?" He's our best trainer of people. Whenever we have an opening and need a good manager, we ring him. He always has somebody who is ready.'

Amazed, the young man thanked Ms. Jones for her time – but on this occasion he got a different response.

'I was glad I could fit you in today', she said. 'The rest of my week is really busy. I wish I knew what the One Minute Manager's secrets were. I've been meaning to go over there and see him, but I just haven't had time.'

Smiling, the young man said, 'I'll give you those secrets as a gift when I find them out myself. Just like he's giving them to me.'

'That would be a precious present', Ms. Jones said with a smile. She looked around her cluttered office and said, 'I could use whatever help I can get'.

The young man left Ms. Jones's office and walked out into the street, shaking his head. The One Minute Manager was absolutely fascinating to him.

That night the young man had a very restless sleep. He found himself excited about the next day – about learning the third secret to becoming a One Minute Manager

THE next morning he arrived at Ms. Brown's office at the stroke of nine. A very smartly dressed woman in her late 50s greeted him. He got the usual, 'He's quite a character, isn't he?' routine, but by now the young man was getting to the point where he could sincerely say, 'Yes, he is!'

'Did he tell you about being a One Minute Manager?' asked Ms. Brown.

'That's all I've been hearing about', the young man said laughing. 'It's not true, is it?' he asked, still wondering if he'd get a different answer.

'You'd better believe it is. I hardly ever see him.'

'You mean you don't have much contact with him', pursued the young man, 'outside your regular weekly meeting?'

'Essentially very little. Except, of course, when I do something wrong', said Ms. Brown.

Shocked, the young man said, 'You mean the only time you see the One Minute Manager is when you do something wrong?'

'Yes. Well, not quite', said Ms. Brown, 'but almost'.

'But I thought a key motto around here was catching people doing things right.'

'It is', insisted Ms. Brown. 'But you have to know some things about me.'

'What?' asked the young man.

'I've been working here for quite a few years. I know this operation inside and out. As a result, the One Minute Manager doesn't have to spend much time with me, if any, on goal setting. In fact, I usually write out my goals and send them over to him.'

'Is each goal on a separate sheet of paper?' asked the young man.

'Indeed it is. No longer than 250 words and each one takes me or the One Minute Manager only a minute to read.

'Another thing about me that's important is that I just love my work. As a result, I do most of my own One Minute Praisings. In fact, I believe if you're not for yourself, who is? A friend of mine told me a motto I'll always remember: "If you don't blow your own horn, someone else will use it as a spittoon".'

The young man smiled. He liked her sense of humour. 'Does your manager ever praise you?' he asked.

'Sometimes he does, but he doesn't have to do it very often because I beat him to the punch', answered Ms. Brown. 'When I do something especially good, I might even ask the One Minute Manager for a praising.'

'How would you ever have the nerve to do that?' asked the young man.

'It's easy. Just like making a bet where I either win or I break even. If he gives me the praising, I win.'

'But if he doesn't?' the young man broke in.

'Then I break even', replied Ms. Brown. 'I didn't have it before I asked.'

The young man smiled as he took note of Ms. Brown's philosophy, and then continued.

'You said he spends time with you when you do something wrong. What do you mean?' asked the young man.

'If I make a significant mistake, that's when I invariably get a One Minute Reprimand', Ms. Brown said.

'A what?' the startled young man asked.

'A One Minute Reprimand', Ms. Brown repeated. 'That's the third secret to becoming a One Minute Manager.'

'How does it work?' wondered the young man out loud.

'It's simple', said Ms. Brown.

'I thought you'd say that', said the young man.

Ms. Brown joined his laugh and explained, 'If you have been doing a job for some time and you know how to do it well, and you make a mistake, the One Minute Manager is quick to respond'.

'What does he do?' asked the young man.

'As soon as he has learned about the mistake he comes to see me. First he confirms the facts. Then he might put his hand on my shoulder or maybe just come round to my side of the desk.'

'Doesn't that bother you?' asked the young man.

'Of course it does, because you know what's coming, especially since he doesn't have a smile on his face.

'He looks me straight in the eye', she continued, 'and tells me precisely what I did wrong. Then he shares with me how he feels about it – he's angry, annoyed, frustrated or whatever he is feeling.'

'How long does that take?' asked the young man.

'Only about 30 seconds but sometimes it seems forever to me', confided Ms. Brown.

The visitor couldn't help but remember how he himself felt when the One Minute Manager told him in no uncertain terms how annoyed he was with his indecision.

'And then what happens?' the young man asked as he moved to the edge of his chair.

'He lets what he said sink in with a few seconds of silence – and does it sink in!'

'Then what?' the young man asked.

'He looks me squarely in the eye and lets me know how competent he thinks I usually am. He makes sure I understand that the only reason he is angry with me is that he has so much respect for me. He says he knows this is so unlike me. He says how much he looks forward to seeing me some other time, as long as I understand that he does not welcome that same mistake again.'

The young man broke in. 'It must make you think twice.'

'It certainly does', Ms. Brown nodded vigorously.

The young man knew what Ms. Brown was talking about. He was taking notes now as fast as he could. He sensed that it wasn't going to take this woman long to cover several important points.

'First of all', Ms. Brown said, 'he usually gives me the reprimand as soon as I've done something wrong. Second, since he specifies exactly what I did wrong, I know he is "on top of things" and that I'm not going to get away with sloppiness. Third, since he doesn't attack me as a person – only my behaviour – it's easier for me not to become defensive. I don't try to rationalize away my mistake by fixing blame on him or somebody else. I know he is being fair. And fourth, he is consistent.'

'Does that mean he will reprimand you for doing something wrong, even if things are going well for him elsewhere?'

'Yes', she answered.

'Does the whole process really take only a minute?' the young man asked.

'Usually', she said. 'And when it's over, it's over. A One Minute Reprimand doesn't last long but I can guarantee you, you don't forget it – and you don't usually make the same mistake twice.'

'I think I know what you're talking about', the young man said. 'I'm afraid I asked him. . . .'

'I hope', she interrupted, 'you didn't ask him to repeat himself'.

The young man was embarrassed. 'I did', he confessed.

'Then you know what it's like to be on the receiving end of a One Minute Reprimand', she said. 'Although I expect, as a visitor. you got a rather mild one.'

'I don't know if you'd call it mild', he said, 'but I don't think I'll ask him to repeat himself very often. That was a mistake.

'I wonder', the visitor continued, 'if the One Minute Manager ever makes a mistake. He seems almost too perfect.'

Ms. Brown began to laugh. 'Hardly', she said. 'But he does have a good sense of humour. So when he does make a mistake, like forgetting to do the last half of the One Minute Reprimand, we point it out to him and kid him about it.

'After we've had time to recover from the Reprimand, that is. We might, for example, phone him later and tell him we know we were wrong. Then we might laugh and ask for the praising half of the Reprimand, because we're not feeling too good.'

'And what does he do then?' the young man asked.

'He usually laughs and says he's sorry he forgot to remind me that I am OK as a person.'

'You can laugh about praisings and reprimands?' the young man asked.

'Of course', Ms. Brown said. 'You see, the One Minute Manager has taught us the value of being able to laugh at ourselves when we make a mistake. It helps us get on with our work.'

'That's terrific', the young man enthused. 'How did you learn to do that?'

'Simply', Ms. Brown answered, 'by watching the boss do it himself'.

'You mean your boss can laugh at himself when he makes a mistake?' the astonished young man asked.

'Well, not always', Ms. Brown admitted. 'He's like most of us. Sometimes it's tough. But he often can. And when he does laugh at himself, it has a positive effect on everyone around him.'

'He must be pretty secure', the young man suggested.

'He is', Ms. Brown answered.

The young man was impressed. He was beginning to see how valuable such a manager was to an organization.

'Why do you think the One Minute Manager's reprimands are so effective?' he asked.

'I'll let you ask the One Minute Manager', she said, as she rose from behind her desk and walked the young man to the door.

When he thanked her for her time, Ms. Brown smiled and said, 'You know what the response to that is going to be'. They both laughed. He was beginning to feel like an 'insider' rather than a visitor, and that felt good.

As soon as he was in the corridor, he realized how little time he'd spent with her and how much information she had given him.

He reflected on what she had said. It sounded so simple. He reviewed in his own mind what you should do when you catch an experienced person doing something wrong.

The One Minute Reprimand works well when you:

1. Tell people *beforehand* that you are going to let them know how they are doing and in no uncertain terms.

The first half of the reprimand:

2. Reprimand people immediately.
3. Tell people what they did wrong – be specific.
4. Tell people how you feel about what they did wrong – and in no uncertain terms.
5. Stop for a few seconds of uncomfortable silence to let them *feel* how you feel.

The second half of the reprimand:

6. Shake hands, or touch them in a way that lets them know you are honestly on their side.
7. Remind them how much you value them.
8. Reaffirm that you think well of them but not of their performance in this situation.
9. Realize that when the reprimand is over, it's over.

The young man would have found it hard to believe in the effectiveness of the One Minute Reprimand if he hadn't personally experienced its effect. There was no doubt that he felt uncomfortable. And he did not want to experience it again.

However, he knew that everyone made mistakes now and then, and that he might very well receive another reprimand some day. But he knew if it came from the One Minute Manager, that it would be fair; that it would be a comment on his behaviour and not on his worth as a person.

As he made his way to the One Minute Manager's office, he kept thinking about the simplicity of One Minute Management.

All three of the secrets made sense – One Minute Goals, One Minute Praisings, and One Minute Reprimands. 'But why do they work?' he wondered. 'Why is the One Minute Manager the most productive manager in the company?'

WHEN he got to the One Minute Manager's office, his secretary said, 'You can go straight in. He's been wondering when you'd be back to see him.'

As the young man entered the office, he noticed again how clear and uncluttered it was. He was greeted by a warm smile from the One Minute Manager.

'Well, what did you find out in your travels?' he asked.

'A lot!' the young man said enthusiastically.

'Tell me what you learned', the manager said encouragingly.

'I found out why you call yourself a One Minute Manager. You set One Minute Goals with your staff to make sure they know what they are being held accountable for and what good performance looks like. You then try to catch them doing something right so you can give them a One Minute Praising. And then, finally, if they have all the skills to do something right and they don't, you give them a One Minute Reprimand.'

'What do you think about all that?' asked the One Minute Manager.

'I'm amazed at how simple it is', said the young man, 'and yet it works – you get results. I'm convinced that it certainly works for you.'

'And it will for you too, if you're willing to *do* it', the manager insisted.

'Perhaps', said the young man, 'but I would be more likely to do it if I could understand more about *why* it works'.

'That's true of everyone, young man. The more you understand why it works, the more apt you are to *use* it. I'd be happy, therefore, to tell you what I know. Where do you want to start?'

'Well, first of all, when you talk about One Minute Management, do you really mean it takes a minute to do all the kinds of things you need to do as a manager?'

'No, not always. It is just a way to say that being a manager is not as complicated as people would have you believe. And also managing people doesn't take as long as you'd think. So when I say One Minute Management, it might take more than a minute for each of the key elements like goal setting, but it's just a symbolic term. And very often it does take only a minute.

'Let me show you one of the notes I keep on my desk.'

When he looked, the young man saw:

*

The Best Minute I Spend Is The One I Invest In People

'It's ironic', the manager said. 'Most companies spend 50 per cent to 70 per cent of their money on people's salaries. And yet they spend less than 1 per cent of their budget to train their people. Most companies, in fact, spend more time and money on maintaining their buildings and equipment than they do on maintaining and developing people.'

'I never thought of that', the young man admitted. 'But if people get results, then it certainly makes good sense to invest in people.'

'Exactly', the manager said. 'I wish someone had invested in me sooner when I first went to work.'

'What do you mean?' the young man asked.

'Well, in most of the organizations I worked in before, I often didn't know what I was supposed to be doing. No one bothered to tell me. If you asked me whether I was doing a good job, I would say either "I don't know" or "I think so". If you asked why I thought so, I would reply, "I haven't been bawled out by my boss lately" or "No news is good news". It was almost as if my main motivation was to avoid punishment.'

'That's interesting', the young man admitted. 'But I'm not sure I understand it.'

Then he added anxiously, 'In fact, if it's all right with you, maybe I could understand things better if I could get to some of my "why" questions. Let's start with One Minute Goal Setting. Why does it work so well?'

'YOU want to know why One Minute Goals work', the manager said. 'Fine.' He got up and began to pace slowly around the room.

'Let me give you an analogy that might help. I've seen a lot of unmotivated people at work in the various organizations I've been employed by over the years. But I've never seen an unmotivated person after work. Everyone seems to be motivated to do something.

'One night, for example, I was bowling and I saw some of the "problem employees" at work from my last organization. One of the real problem people, whom I remembered all too well, took the bowling ball and approached the line and rolled the ball. Then he started to scream and yell and jump around. Why do you think he was so happy?'

'Because he got a strike. He had knocked down all the pins.'

'Exactly. Why don't you think he and other people are that excited at work?'

'Because he doesn't know where the pins are', smiled the young man. 'I get it. How long would he want to bowl if there were no pins?'

'Right', said the One Minute Manager. 'Now you can see what happens in most organizations. I believe that most managers know what they want their people to do. They just don't bother to tell their people in a way they would understand. They assume they should know. I never assume anything when it comes to goal setting.

'When you assume that people know what's expected of them, you are creating an ineffective form of bowling. You put the pins up but when the bowler goes to roll the ball, he notices there is a sheet across the pins. So when he rolls the ball, and it slips under the sheet, he hears a crack but doesn't know how many pins he's knocked down. When you ask him how he did, he says, *I don't know. But it felt good.*

'It's like playing golf at night. A lot of my friends have given up golf and when I asked them why, they said, "Because the courses are too crowded". When I suggested that they play at night, they laughed because who would ever play golf without being able to see the greens?

'It's the same with watching football. How many people in this country would sit in front of their television sets and watch two teams run up and down the field if there were no goals to shoot at or any way to score?'

'Yes! Why is that?' asked the young man.

'It's all because clearly the number one motivator of people is feedback on results. In fact, we have another saying here that's worth noting: *"Feedback is the Breakfast of Champions"*. Feedback keeps us going. Unfortunately, however, when most managers realize that feedback on results is the number one motivator of people, they usually set up a third form of bowling.

'When the bowler goes to the line to roll the ball, the pins are still up and the sheet is in place but now there is another ingredient in the game - a supervisor standing behind the sheet. When the bowler rolls the ball, he hears the crash of the falling pins, and the supervisor holds up two fingers to signify you knocked down two pins. Actually, do most managers say you got two?'

'No', the young man smiled. 'They usually say you missed eight.'

Right!' said the One Minute Manager. 'The question I always used to ask was why the manager doesn't lift up the sheet so both he and his subordinate can see the pins. Why? Because he has the Annual Performance Review coming up.'

'Because he has Performance Review coming up?' wondered the young man.

'Yes. Such managers don't tell their people what they expect of them; they just leave them alone and then tear them off a ctrip when they don't perform at the desired level.'

'Why do you suppose they would do that?' the young man inquired, being very familiar with the truth in the manager's comments.

'So they can look good', said the manager.

'What do you mean, so they can look good?' asked the young man.

'How do you think you would be viewed by your boss if you rated everyone that reported to you at the highest level on your performance review scale?'

'As a "soft touch", as someone who could not discriminate between good performance and poor performance.'

'Precisely', said the manager. 'In order to look good as a manager in most organizations, you have to catch some of your people doing things wrong. You have to have a few winners, a few losers, and everyone else somewhere in the middle. You see, in this country we have a normal-distribution-curve mentality. I remember one time when visiting my son's school, I watched a teacher giving a geography test to her class. When I asked her why she didn't put atlases around the room and let the kids use them during the test, she said, "I couldn't do that because all the kids would get 100 per cent". As though it would be bad for everyone to do well.

'I remember once reading that when someone asked Einstein what his phone number was, he went to the phone book to look it up.'

The young man laughed. 'You're kidding.'

'No, I'm not kidding. He said he never cluttered his mind with information he could find somewhere else.

'Now, if you didn't know better', the manager continued, 'what would you think of someone who went to the phone book to look up his own number? Would you think he was a winner or a loser?'

The young man grinned and said, 'A real loser'.

'Of course you would', the manager said. 'I would, too, but we'd be wrong, wouldn't we?'

The young man nodded his agreement.

'It's easy for any of us to make this mistake', the manager said. Then he showed his visitor the plaque he had made for himself. 'Look at this':

*

Everyone
Is A Potential Winner

Some People
Are Disguised
As Losers,

Don't Let
Their Appearances
Fool You

*

'You see', the manager said, 'you really have three choices as a manager. First, you can hire winners. They are hard to find and they cost money. Or, second, if you can't find a winner, you can hire someone with the potential to be a winner. Then you systematically train that person to become a winner. If you are not willing to do either of the first two (and I am continually amazed at the number of managers who won't spend the money to hire a winner or take the time to train someone to become a winner), then there is only the third choice left – prayer.'

That stopped the young man cold. He put down his notebook and pen and said, 'Prayer?'

The manager laughed quietly. 'That's just my attempt at humour, young man. But when you think about it, there are many managers who are saying their prayers daily – "I hope this person works out".'

'Oh', the young man said seriously. 'Well, let's take the first choice. If you hire a winner, it's really easy to be a One Minute Manager, isn't it?'

'It certainly is', said the manager with a smile. He was amazed at how serious the young man was now – as though being more serious made a person a better manager. 'All you have to do with a winner is do One Minute Goal Setting and let them run with the ball.'

'I understand from Ms. Brown that sometimes you don't even have to do that with her', said the young man.

'She's absolutely right', said the manager. 'She's forgotten more than most people know around here. But with everyone, winner or potential winner, One Minute Goal Setting is a basic tool for productive behaviour.'

'Is it true that no matter who initiates the One Minute Goal Setting', the young man asked, 'each goal always has to be written down on a single sheet of paper?'

'Absolutely', insisted the One Minute Manager.

'Why is that so important?'

'So people can review their goals frequently and then check their performance against those goals.'

'I understand you insist they write down only their major goals and responsibilities and not every aspect of their job', the young man said.

'Yes. That's because I don't want this to be a paper mill. I don't want a lot of pieces of paper filed away somewhere and looked at only once a year when it's time for next year's goal setting or performance review, or some such thing.

'As you probably saw, everyone who works for me has a plaque near them that looks like this.' He showed his visitor his copy of the plaque.

*

Take A Minute:

Look At Your Goals

Look At
Your Performance

See If Your Behaviour
Matches Your Goals

*

The young man was amazed. He'd missed this in his brief visit. 'I never saw this', he said. 'It's terrific. Could I get one of these plaques?'

'Of course', the manager said. 'I'll arrange it.'

As he was writing down some of what he was learning, the aspiring manager said, without lifting up his head, 'You know, it's difficult to learn everything there is to learn about One Minute Management in such a short time. There's certainly more I'd like to learn about One Minute Goals, for instance, but maybe I could do that later.

'Could we move to One Minute Praisings now?' asked the young man, as he looked up from his notebook.

'Certainly', said the One Minute Manager. 'You're probably wondering why that works, too.'

'Indeed I am', the visitor responded.

'LET'S look at a fewexamples', the One Minute Manager said. 'Maybe then it will be clear to you why One Minute Praisings work so well.'

'I'd like that', said the young man.

'I'll start with a pigeon example and then move on to people', said the manager. 'Just remember, though, that people are not pigeons. People are more complicated. They are aware, they think for themselves and they certainly don't want to be manipulated by another person. Remember that and respect that. It is a key to good management.

'With that in mind, let us look at several simple examples which show us that we all seek what feels good to us and we avoid what feels bad to us.

'Suppose you have an untrained pigeon that you want to enter a box in the lower left-hand corner and run across the box to the upper right-hand corner and push a lever with his right foot. Suppose that not too far from the entry point we have a pellet machine – that is, a machine that can release pellets of food to reward and reinforce the pigeon. What do you think is going to happen if we put the pigeon in the box and wait until the pigeon runs over to the upper right-hand corner and pushes the lever with his right foot before we give him any food?' asked the One Minute Manager.

'He would starve to death', responded the young man.

'You're right. We're going to lose a lot of pigeons. The pigeon is going to starve to death because he has no idea what he is supposed to do.

'Now it's actually not too hard to train a pigeon to do this task. All you have to do is to draw a line not too far from where the pigeon enters the box. If the pigeon enters the box and crosses the line – bang – the pellet machine goes off and the pigeon gets fed. Pretty soon you have the pigeon running to that spot, but you don't want the pigeon there. Where do you want the pigeon?'

'In the upper right-hand corner of the box', said the young man.

'Right!' said the One Minute Manager. 'Therefore, after a while you stop rewarding the pigeon for running to that spot and draw another line which isn't too far from the last line, but is in the direction of the goal – the upper right-hand corner of the box. Now the pigeon starts running around his old spot and doesn't get fed. Pretty soon, though, the pigeon makes it across the new line and – bang – the machine goes off again and the pigeon gets fed.

'Then you draw another line. Again this line has to be in the direction of the goal, but not so far away that the pigeon can't make it again. We keep setting up these lines closer and closer to the upper right-hand corner of the box until we won't feed the pigeon unless he hits the lever, and then finally only when he hits the lever with his right foot.'

'Why do you set up all these little goals?' wondered the young man.

'By setting up these series of lines, we are establishing goals that the pigeon can achieve. So the key to training someone to do a new task is, in the beginning, to catch them doing something approximately right until they can eventually learn to do it exactly right.

'We use this concept all the time with kids and animals, but we somehow forget it when we are dealing with adults. For example, at some of these sea aquarium shows you see around the country, the show usually ends with a huge whale jumping over a rope which is high above the water. When the whale comes down he drenches the first ten rows.

'The people leave that show mumbling to themselves, "That's unbelievable. How do they teach that whale to do that?"

'Do you think they go out in the ocean in a boat', the manager asked, 'and put a rope out over the water and yell, "Up, up!" until a whale jumps out of the water over the rope? And then say, "Hey, let's hire him. He's a real winner".'

'No', laughed the young man, 'but that really *would* be hiring a winner'.

The two men enjoyed the laugh they shared.

'You're right', the manager said. 'When they captured the whale, he knew nothing about jumping over ropes. So when they began to train him in the large pool, where do you think they started the rope?'

'At the bottom of the pool', answered the young man.

'Of course!' retorted the manager. 'Every time the whale swam over the rope – which was every time he swam past – he got fed. Soon, they raised the rope a little.

'If the whale swam under the rope, he didn't get fed during training. Whenever he swam over the rope, he got fed. So after a while the whale started swimming over the rope all the time. Then they started raising the rope a little higher.'

'Why do they raise the rope?' asked the young man.

'First', the manager began, 'because they were clear on the goal: to get the whale to jump high out of the water and over the rope.

'And second', the One Minute Manager pointed out, 'it's not a very exciting show for a trainer to say, "Look, everyone, the whale did it again". Everybody may be looking in the water but they can't see anything. Over a period of time they keep on raising the rope until they finally get it to the surface of the water. Now the whale knows that, in order to get fed, he has to jump partially out of the water and over the rope. As soon as that goal is reached, they can start raising the rope higher and higher out of the water.'

'So that's how they do it', the young man said. 'Well, I can understand now how using that method works with animals, but isn't it a bit much to use it with people?'

'No, it's very natural, in fact', the manager said. 'We all do essentially the same thing with the children we care for. How do you think you teach them to walk? Can you imagine standing a child up and saying "Walk", and when he falls down you pick him up and spank him and say, "I told you to walk". No, you stand the child up and the first day he wobbles a little bit, and you get all excited and say, "He stood, he stood", and you hug and kiss the child. The next day he stands for a moment and maybe wobbles a step and you are all over him with kisses and hugs.

'Finally the child, realizing that this is a pretty good deal, starts to wobble his legs more and more until he eventually walks.

'The same thing goes for teaching a child to speak. Suppose you wanted a child to say, "Give me a glass of water, please". If you waited until the child said the whole sentence before you gave her any water, the child would die of thirst. So you start off by saying "Water, water". All of a sudden one day the child says, "Waller". You jump all over the place, hug and kiss the child, and get grandmother on the phone so the child can say "Waller, waller". That wasn't "water", of course, but it was close.

'Now you don't want a kid going into a restaurant at the age of twenty-one asking for a glass of "waller" so after a while you accept only the word "water" and then you begin on "please".

'These examples illustrate that the most important thing in training somebody to become a winner is to catch them doing something right – in the beginning approximately right and gradually moving them towards the desired behaviour. With a winner you don't have to catch them doing things right very often, because good performers catch themselves doing things right and are able to be self-reinforcing.'

'Is that why you observe new staff a lot in the beginning', asked the young man, 'or when your more experienced people are starting a new project?'

'Yes', the One Minute Manager said. 'Most managers wait until their staff do something exactly right before they praise them. As a result, many people never get to become high performers because their managers concentrate on catching them doing things wrong – that is, anything that falls short of the final desired performance. In our pigeon example, it would be like putting the pigeon in the box and not only waiting until he hits the lever to give him any food but putting some electric grilles around the box to punish him periodically just to keep him motivated.'

'That doesn't sound as though it would be very effective', the young man suggested.

'Well, it isn't', agreed the One Minute Manager. 'After getting punished for a while and not knowing what acceptable behaviour is (that is, hitting the lever), the pigeon would go into the corner of the box and not move. To the pigeon it is a hostile environment and not worth taking any risks in.

'That is what we often do with new, inexperienced people. We welcome them aboard, take them around to meet everybody, and then we leave them alone. Not only do we not catch them doing anything approximately right, but periodically we haul them over the coals just to keep them moving. This is the most popular leadership style of all. We call it the "leave alone–rebuke" style. You leave a person alone, expecting good performance from them, and when you don't get it, you rebuke them.'

'What happens to these people?' asked the young man.

'If you've been in any organization, and I understand you've visited several', the manager said, 'you know, because you've seen them. They do as little as possible.

'And that's what's wrong with most businesses today. Their people really do not produce – either quantity or quality.

'And much of the reason for this poor business performance is simply because the people are managed so poorly.'

The young man put down his notebook. He thought about what he just heard. He was beginning to see One Minute Management for what it is – a practical business tool.

It was amazing to him how well something as simple as the One Minute Praising worked – whether it was inside or outside the business world.

'That reminds me of some friends of mine', the young man said. 'They rang me and said that they'd bought a new dog. They asked me what I thought of their planned method for training the dog.'

The manager was almost afraid to ask, 'How were they going to do it?'

'They said if the dog had an accident on the carpet, they were going to take the dog, shove his nose in it, hit him with a newspaper and then throw him out of this little window in the kitchen into the garden – where the dog was supposed to do his job.

'Then, they asked me what I thought would happen with this method. I laughed because I knew what would happen. After about three days the dog would poop on the floor and jump out the window. The dog didn't know what to do, but he knew he had better clear the area.'

The manager roared his approval.

'That's a great story', he said. 'You see, that's what punishment does when you use it with somebody who lacks confidence or is insecure because of lack of experience. If inexperienced people don't perform (that is, do what you want them to do), then rather than punish them we need to go back to One Minute Goal Setting and make sure they understand what is expected of them, and that they have seen what good performance looks like.'

'Well, then, after you have done One Minute Goal Setting again', the young man asked, 'do you try to catch them doing something approximately right again?'

'Precisely so', the One Minute Manager agreed. 'You're always trying to create situations in the beginning where you can give a One Minute Praising.' Then, looking the young man straight in the eyes, the manager said, 'You are a very enthusiastic and receptive learner. That makes me pleased to be sharing the secrets of One Minute Management with you.' They both smiled. They knew a One Minute Praising when they heard one.

'I certainly prefer a praising to a reprimand', the young man laughed.

'I think I understand now why One Minute Goals and One Minute Praisings work. They really do make good sense to me.'

'Good', said the One Minute Manager.

'But I can't imagine why the One Minute Reprimand works', the young man wondered out loud.

'Let me tell you a few things about it', said the One Minute Manager.

'THERE are several reasons why the One Minute Reprimand works so well.

'To begin with', the manager explained, 'the feedback in the One Minute Reprimand is immediate. That is, you get to the individual as soon as you observe the "misbehaviour" or your data information system tips you off. It is not appropriate to save up negative feelings about someone's poor performance.

'The fact that the feedback is so immediate is an important lesson in why the One Minute Reprimand works so well. Unless discipline occurs as soon after the misbehaviour as possible, it tends not to be as helpful in influencing future behaviour. Most managers store up observations of poor behaviour and then some day when performance review comes or they are angry in general, they charge in and let fly with a long list of misdemeanours. They tell people all the things they have done wrong for the last few weeks or months or more.'

The young man breathed a deep sigh and said, 'So true'.

'And then', the One Minute Manager went on, 'the manager and subordinate usually end up yelling at each other about the facts or simply keeping quiet and resenting each other. The person receiving the feedback doesn't really hear what he or she has done wrong. This is a version of the "leave alone-rebuke" form of discipline that I've spoken about earlier.'

'I remember it well', responded the young man. 'That is certainly something I want to avoid.'

'Absolutely', agreed the manager. 'If managers would only intervene early, they could deal with one behaviour at a time and the person receiving the discipline would not be overwhelmed. They could hear the feedback. That's why I think performance review is an ongoing process, not something you do only once a year.'

'So, one reason that the One Minute Reprimand works is that the person receiving the reprimand can "hear" the feedback, because when the manager deals with one behaviour at a time, it seems more fair and clear', the young man summarized.

'Yes', the manager said. 'And secondly, when I give a One Minute Reprimand, I never attack a person's value as a person. Since their worth as a person is not on the line, they don't feel they have to defend themselves. I reprimand the *behaviour* only. Thus, my feedback and their own reaction to it is about the specific behaviour and not their feelings about themselves as human beings.

'So often, when disciplining people, managers persecute the individual. My purpose in a One Minute Reprimand is to eliminate the behaviour and keep the person.'

'So that's why you make the second half of the reprimand a praising', the young man said. 'Their behaviour is not all right. They are all right.'

'Yes', agreed the One Minute Manager.

'Why wouldn't you give the praising first and then the reprimand?' suggested the young man.

'For some reason, it just doesn't work', insisted the manager. 'Some people, now that I think of it, say that I am nice and tough as a manager. But to be more accurate, I'm really tough and nice.'

'Tough and nice', echoed the young man.

'Yes', insisted the One Minute Manager. 'This is an old philosophy that has worked well for literally thousands of years.

'There is, in fact, a story in ancient China that illustrates this. Once upon a time, an emperor appointed a second in command. He called this prime minister in and, in effect, said to him, *Why don't we divide up the tasks? Why don't you do all the punishing and I'll do all the rewarding?* The prime minister said, *Fine. I'll do all the punishing and you do all the rewarding.*'

'I think I'm going to like this story', the young man said.

'You will, you will', the One Minute Manager replied with a knowing smile.

'Now this emperor', the manager continued, 'soon noticed that whenever he asked someone to do something, they might do it or they might not do it. However, when the prime minister spoke, people moved. So the emperor called in the prime minister again and said, *Why don't we divide the tasks again? You have been doing all the punishing here for quite a while. Now let me do the punishing and you do the rewarding.* So the prime minister and the emperor switched roles again.

'And, within a month, the prime minister was emperor. The emperor had been a nice person, rewarding and being kind to everyone; then he started to punish people. People said, *What's wrong with that old codger?* and they threw him out on his ear. When they came to look for a replacement, they said, *You know who's really starting to come around now – the prime minister.* So they put him into office.'

'Is that a true story?' the young man asked.

'Who cares?' said the One Minute Manager, laughing. 'Seriously', he added, 'I do know this. If you are first tough on the behaviour, and *then* supportive of the person, it works.'

'Do you have any modern-day examples of where the One Minute Reprimand has worked other than in management?' the young man asked the manager.

'Yes, certainly', the manager said. 'Let me mention two: one with severe adult behaviour problems and another in disciplining children.'

'What do you mean when you say "severe adult behaviour problems"?' the young man asked.

'I'm talking about alcoholics in particular', the manager answered. 'About thirty years ago an observant clergyman discovered a technique which is now called "crisis intervention". He made the discovery when he was helping a physician's wife. She had been taken to hospital in a critical condition and was slowly dying from cirrhosis of the liver. But she was still denying that she had a drinking problem. When all her family had gathered at her bedside, the clergyman asked each of them to describe specific drinking incidents they had observed. That's an important part of the One Minute Reprimand. Before giving a reprimand you have to see the behaviour yourself - you can't depend on what someone else saw. You never give a reprimand based on hearsay.'

'Interesting', the young man broke in.

'Let me finish. After the family described specific behaviours, the clergyman asked each of the family members to tell the woman how they felt about those incidents. Gathered closely around her, one by one they told her first what she *did*, and second, how they *felt* about it. They were angry, frustrated, embarrassed. And then they told her how much they loved her, and they instinctively touched her and gently said how they wanted her to live and to enjoy life once again. That was why they were so angry with her.'

'That sounds so simple', said the young man, 'especially with something as complicated as a drinking problem. Did it work?'

'Amazingly so', the One Minute Manager insisted. 'It's not as simple as I've summarized it, of course. But these three basic ingredients – telling people what they did wrong; telling people how you feel about it; and reminding people that they are valuable and worthwhile – lead to significant improvements in people's behaviour.'

'That's nothing short of incredible', the young man said.

'I know it is', the manager agreed.

'You said you'd give me two examples of how other people successfully use methods like the One Minute Reprimand', the young man said.

'Yes, of course. In the early 1970s, a family psychiatrist in California also made the same amazing discovery with children. He had read a lot about bonding – the emotional ties people have to people. He knew what people needed. People need to be in contact with people who care about them – to be accepted as valuable just because they are people.

'The doctor also knew that people need to have a spade called a spade – to be pulled up short by people who care when they are not behaving well.'

'How does that translate', the young man wanted to know, 'into practical action?'

'Each parent is taught to physically touch their child by putting their hand on the child's shoulder, touching his arm or, if he is young, actually sitting the child on their lap. Then the parent tells the child exactly what he did wrong and how the parent feels about it – and in no uncertain terms. (You can see that this is very like what the family members did for the sick woman.) Finally, the parent takes a deep breath, and allows for a few seconds of silence – so the child can *feel* whatever the parent is feeling. Then the parent tells the youngster how valuable and important the child is to the parent.

'You see, it is very important when you are managing people to remember that behaviour and worth are not the same things. What is really worthwhile is the *person* managing their own behaviour. This is as true of each of us as managers as it is of each of the people we are managing.

'In fact, if you know this', the manager said, as he pointed to one of his favourite plaques, 'you will know the key to a really successful reprimand'.

*

We Are Not
Just
Our Behaviour

We Are
The Person
Managing
Our Behaviour

*

'If you realize that you are managing people, and not just their recent behaviour', the manager concluded, 'you will do well'.

'It sounds as though there's a lot of caring and respect behind such a reprimand', the young man said.

'I'm glad you noticed that, young man. You will be successful with the One Minute Reprimand when you really care about the welfare of the person you are reprimanding.'

'That reminds me', the young man said, 'Mr. Levy told me that you pat him on the shoulder, or shake hands, or in some other way make contact with him during a praising. And now I notice that the parents are encouraged to touch their children during the scolding. Is touching an important part of the One Minute Praisings and Reprimands?'

'Yes and no', the manager answered with a smile. 'Yes, if you know the person well and are clearly interested in helping the person to succeed in his or her work. And no, if you or the other person has any doubts about that.

'Touch is a very powerful message', the manager pointed out. 'People have strong feelings about being touched, and that needs to be respected. Would you, for instance, like someone whose motives you weren't sure of to touch you during a praising or a reprimand?'

'No', the young man answered clearly. 'I really wouldn't!'

'You see what I mean', the manager explained. 'Touch is very honest. People know immediately when you touch them whether you care about them, or whether you are just trying to find a new way to manipulate them.

'There is a very simple rule about touching', the manager continued. '*When you touch, don't take.* Touch the people you manage only when you are *giving* them something – reassurance, support, encouragement, or whatever.'

'So you should refrain from touching someone', the young man said, 'until you know them and they know you are interested in their success – that you are clearly on their side. I can see that.

'But', the young man continued hesitantly, 'while the One Minute Praisings and the One Minute Reprimands look simple enough, aren't they really just powerful ways for you to get people to do what you want them to do? And isn't that manipulative?'

'You are right about One Minute Management being a powerful way to get people to do what you want them to do', the manager confirmed.

'However, manipulation is getting people to do something they are either *not aware of* or *don't agree to.* That is why it is so important to let each person know *right from the start* what you are doing and why.

'It's like anything else in life', the manager explained. 'There are things that work, and things that don't work. Being honest with people eventually works. On the other hand, as you have probably learned in your own life, being dishonest eventually leads to failing with people. It's just that simple.'

'I can see now', the young man said, 'where the power of your management style comes from – you care about people'.

'Yes', the manager said simply, 'I do'.

The young man remembered how gruff he thought this special manager was when he first met him.

It was as though the manager could read his mind.

'Sometimes', the One Minute Manager said, 'you have to care enough to be tough. And I am. I am very tough on the poor performance – but only on the performance. I am never tough on the person.'

The young man liked the One Minute Manager. He knew now why people liked to work with him.

'Maybe you would find this interesting', the younger man said, as he pointed to his notebook. 'It is a plaque I've created to remind me of how *goals* – the One Minute Goals – and *consequences* – the Praisings and the Reprimands – affect people's behaviour.'

*

Goals
Begin
Behaviours

Consequences
Maintain
Behaviours

*

'That's very good!' the manager exclaimed.

'Do you think so?' the young man asked, wanting to hear the compliment once again.

'Young man', the manager said very slowly for emphasis, 'it is not my role in life to be a human tape recorder. I do not have time to continually repeat myself.'

Just when he thought he would be praised, the young man felt he was in for another One Minute Reprimand, something he wanted to avoid.

The bright young man kept a straight face and said simply, 'What did you say?'

They looked at each other only for a moment and then they both started to laugh.

'I like you, young man', the manager said. 'How would you like to go to work here?'

The young man put down his notebook and stared in amazement. 'You mean go to work for you?' he asked enthusiastically.

'No. I mean go to work for yourself like the other people in my department. Nobody ever really works for anybody else. I just help people work better and in the process they benefit our organization.'

This was, of course, what the young man had been looking for all along.

'I'd love to work here', he said.

And so he did – for some time.

The time the special manager had invested in him paid off. Because eventually, the inevitable happened.

HE became a One Minute Manager.

He became a One Minute Manager not because he thought like one, or talked like one, but because he behaved like one.

He set One Minute Goals.

He gave One Minute Praisings.

He gave One Minute Reprimands.

He asked brief, important questions; spoke the simple truth; laughed, worked, and enjoyed.

And, perhaps most important of all, he encouraged the people he worked with to do the same.

He had even created a pocket-sized 'Game Plan' to make it easier for the people around him to become One Minute Managers. He had given it as a useful gift to each person who reported to him.

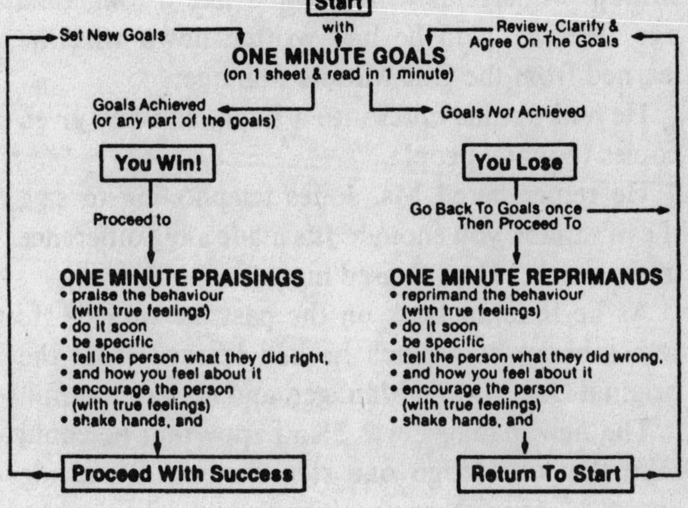
A very brief summary of
THE ONE MINUTE MANAGER'S "GAME PLAN"
How to give yourself & others 'the gift' of getting greater results in less time.
SET GOALS; PRAISE & REPRIMAND BEHAVIOURS; ENCOURAGE PEOPLE;
SPEAK THE TRUTH; LAUGH; WORK; ENJOY
and encourage the people you work with to do the same as you do!
Start
with
Set New Goals
Review, Clarify & Agree On The Goals
ONE MINUTE GOALS
(on 1 sheet & read in 1 minute)
Goals Achieved
(or any part of the goals)
Goals Not Achieved
You Win!
You Lose
Proceed to
Go Back To Goals once
Then Proceed To
ONE MINUTE PRAISINGS
• praise the behaviour
(with true feelings)
• do it soon
• be specific
• tell the person what they did right,
• and how you feel about it
• encourage the person
(with true feelings)
• shake hands, and
ONE MINUTE REPRIMANDS
• reprimand the behaviour
(with true feelings)
• do it soon
• be specific
• tell the person what they did wrong,
• and how you feel about it
• encourage the person
(with true feelings)
• shake hands, and
Proceed With Success
Return To Start

MANY years later, the man looked back on the time when he first heard of the principles of One Minute Management. It seemed like a long time ago. He was glad he had written down what he learned from the One Minute Manager.

He had put his notes into a book, and had given copies to many people.

He remembered Ms. Jones telephoning to say, 'I can't thank you enough. It's made a big difference in my work.' That pleased him.

As he thought back on the past, he smiled. He remembered how much he had learned from the original One Minute Manager, and he was grateful.

The new manager was also happy that he could take the knowledge one step further. By giving copies to many other people in the organization, he had solved several practical problems.

Everyone who worked with him felt secure. No one felt manipulated or threatened because everyone knew right from the start what he was doing and why.

They could also see *why* the seemingly simple One Minute Management techniques - Goals, Praising and Reprimands - worked so well with people.

Every person who had their own copy of the text could read and re-read it at their own pace until they could understand it and put it to good use themselves. The manager knew full well the very practical advantage of repetition in learning anything new.

Sharing the knowledge in this simple and honest way had, of course, saved him a good deal of time. And it had certainly made his job easier.

Many of the people reporting to him had become One Minute Managers themselves. And they, in turn, had done the same for many of the people who reported to them.

The entire organization had become more effective.

As he sat at his desk thinking, the new One Minute Manager realized what a fortunate individual he was. He had given himself the gift of getting greater results in less time.

He had time to think and to plan – to give his organization the kind of help it needed.

He had time to exercise and stay healthy.

He knew he did not experience the daily emotional and physical stress other managers subjected themselves to.

And he knew that many of the other people who worked with him enjoyed the same benefits.

His department had fewer costly personnel turnovers, less personal illness, and less absenteeism. The benefits were significant.

Then he got up from his desk and began to walk about his uncluttered office. He was deep in thought.

He felt good about himself – as a person and as a manager.

His caring about people had paid off handsomely. He had risen in the organization, gaining more responsibilities and more rewards.

And he knew he had become an effective manager, because both his organization and the people in it had clearly benefited from his presence.

SUDDENLY the intercom buzzed and startled the man. 'Excuse me for interrupting you', he heard his secretary say, 'but there is a young woman on the phone. She wants to know if she can come and talk to you about the way we manage people here.'

The new One Minute Manager was pleased. He knew more women were entering the business world. And he was glad that some of them were as keen to learn about good management as he had been.

The manager's department was now running smoothly. As you might expect, it was one of the best operations of its kind in the world. The members of his staff were productive and happy. And he was happy too. It felt good to be in his position.

'Come any time', he heard himself telling the caller.

And soon he found himself talking to a bright young person. 'I'm glad to share my management secrets with you', the new One Minute Manager said, as he showed the visitor to a seat. 'I will only make one request of you.'

'What's that?' the visitor asked.

'Simply', the manager began, 'that you:'

*

Share It With Others

*

Acknowledgments

Over the years we have learned from, and been influenced by, many individuals. We would like to acknowledge and give a public praising to the following people:

A Special Praising to:

**Dr. Gerald Nelson*, the originator of The One Minute Scolding, an amazingly effective method of parental discipline. We have adapted his method into 'The One Minute Reprimand', an equally effective method of *managerial* discipline. Dr. Nelson is also co-author of *The One Minute Scolding*.

and to:

Dr. Elliott Carlisle for what he taught us about productive managers who have time to think and plan.

Dr. Thomas Connellan for what he taught us about making behavioural concepts and theories clear and understandable to all.

Dr. Paul Hersey for what he taught us about weaving the various applied behavioural sciences into a useful fabric.

Dr. Vernon Johnson for what he taught us about the Crisis Intervention Method of treatment for alcoholics.

Dr. Dorothy Jongeward, *Jay Shelov*, and *Abe Wagner* for what they taught us about communication and the worth of people *as* people.

Dr. Robert Lorber for what he taught us about the application and use of behavioural concepts in business and industry.

Dr. Kenneth Majer for what he taught us about goal-setting and performance.

Dr. Charles McCormick for what he taught us about touching and professionalism.

Dr. Carl Rogers for what he taught us about personal honesty and openness.

Louis Tice for what he taught us about unlocking human potential.

About the Authors

Dr. Kenneth Blanchard, President of Blanchard Training and Development, Inc. (BTD), is an internationally known author, educator and consultant/trainer. He is the co-author of the highly acclaimed and most widely used text on leadership and organization behaviour, *Management of Organization Behaviour: Utilizing Human Resources*, which is in its fourth edition and has been translated into numerous languages.

Dr. Blanchard received his B.A. from Cornell University in Government and Philosophy, an M.A. from Colgate University in Sociology and Counselling and a Ph.D. from Cornell in Administration and Management. He presently serves as a professor of Leadership and Organizational Behaviour at University of Massachusetts, Amherst. In addition, he is a member of the National Training Laboratories (NTL).

Dr. Blanchard has advised such distinguished corporations and agencies as Chevron, Lockheed, AT&T, Holiday Inns, Young Presidents' Organization, the United States Armed Forces, and UNESCO. The Hersey/Blanchard Situational Leadership approach to management has been incorporated into the training and development programmes of Mobil Oil, Caterpillar, Union 76, IBM, Xerox, The Southland Corporation, and numerous fast-growing entrepreneurial companies. In his role as management consultant, Dr. Blanchard teaches seminars throughout America. He is president of Blanchard Training and Development, Inc., in Escondido, California.

Dr. Spencer Johnson is the Chairman of Candle Communications Corporation, and an active author, publisher, lecturer and communications consultant. He has written more than a dozen books dealing with medicine and psychology, and has over three million copies of his books in print.

Dr. Johnson's education includes a degree in psychology from the University of Southern California, an M.D. degree from the Royal College of Surgeons in Ireland, and medical clerkships at Harvard Medical School and the Mayo Clinic.

He has been Medical Director of Communications for Medtronic, a pioneering manufacturer of cardiac pacemakers, and Research Physician for the Institute For Interdisciplinary Studies, a medical-social think-tank in Minneapolis. He has also served as a consultant in communications for the Centre for the Study of the Person, Human Dimensions in Medicine Programme; and to the Office of Continuing Education at the School of Medicine, University of California in La Jolla, California.

One of his recent books, *The Precious Present*, has been praised by the eminent psychologist Dr. Carl Rogers, and by Dr. Norman Vincent Peale, who states, 'What a change might take place if everyone would read this book and apply the principles it teaches'.

The One Minute Manager, like all the other books Dr. Johnson has written, reflects his continuing interest in helping people to experience less stress and better health through better communications. Dr. Johnson and Dr. Blanchard have also produced, in conjunction with 20th Century-Fox, *The One Minute Manager* videotape.